Gulliver's Travels

JONATHAN SWIFT

Level 2

Retold by Pauline Francis
Series Editors: Andy Hopkins and Jocelyn Potter

Pearson Education Limited
Edinburgh Gate, Harlow,
Essex CM20 2JE, England
and Associated Companies throughout the world.

ISBN: 978-1-4058-4284-6

First published by Penguin Books 2000
This edition published 2008

7 9 10 8 6

Text copyright © Penguin Books Ltd 2000
This edition copyright © Pearson Education Ltd 2008
Illustrations by Victor Ambrus

Typeset by Graphicraft Ltd, Hong Kong
Set in 11/14pt Bembo
Printed in China
SWTC/06

Published by Pearson Education Ltd in association with
Penguin Books Ltd, both companies being subsidiaries of Pearson Plc

For a complete list of the titles available in the Penguin Readers series please write to your local
Pearson Longman office or to: Penguin Readers Marketing Department, Pearson Education,
Edinburgh Gate, Harlow, Essex CM20 2JE, England.

Contents

Introduction

Then something moved on my foot. It moved over my body and up to my face. I looked down and I saw a man. He was smaller than my hand. Forty more little men followed him.

This is Gulliver in Lilliput. He travels across the sea from England and has an accident. He arrives in a country of very, very small people. What will they do with him? How will he talk to them? And why are the Big-enders fighting the Little-enders? Is their fight *really* important?

Readers know that the stories about the country of Lilliput and the other countries in *Gulliver's Travels* are not true. But when we read the book, we see our world through the eyes of the little people – and later, through the eyes of big people and horses.

Swift wants us to think about our ideas and our lives, and perhaps to change them. But at the same time, we enjoy the stories. Children like them because they are clever and funny. But *Gulliver's Travels* is for people of all ages. Swift wanted everybody to learn from his book.

Jonathan Swift was born in Dublin, Ireland, in 1667. He went to university – to Trinity College, Dublin – and after that he worked for a writer in London. Then he wrote too.

Swift wrote well about the ideas of his time. But some people did not like his new ideas, and in 1714 Swift went back to Ireland. He wanted to help the Irish people, and he wrote about the English in Ireland. They were often unkind, people felt. At the same time, Swift wrote *Gulliver's Travels*. The book was in the shops in 1726 – and it is there now.

PART 1   A JOURNEY TO LILLIPUT

Chapter 1   I Come to Lilliput

My father lived in the north of England, but he was not very rich. I was the youngest of five brothers. I left school when I was seventeen years old. My father could not pay for me after that. I travelled on the ship *Antelope* to the South Seas. We left Bristol in May, 1699.

I will not write down everything about our journey on those seas. But I will tell you this. On our way to the East Indies, a great wind carried us the wrong way. Twelve of our men died from the hard work and bad food, and the other men were not very strong.

One morning there was heavy rain and we could not see well. In the strong winds, the ship hit something in the water, and broke. Six of us got a boat into the sea. But we were weak and the wind turned it over. We fell into the water.

The wind and the water carried me away from the other men and I never saw them again.

'I'm going to die!' I cried loudly.

But then I put my feet down. I could stand! The wind was weaker now. I walked for more than a kilometre through the water and came to an island. It was after seven at night. I travelled another half a kilometre, but there were no houses or people. Perhaps I could not see them because I was very tired. Then I sat on the ground and slept the best sleep of my life.

◆

I woke up after about nine hours. It was daylight and I was on my back. I tried to stand up, but I could not move! I turned my

I travelled on the ship Antelope *to the South Seas.*

head a little and looked round me. I saw thousands of strings across my body. They were everywhere – round my arms, my feet and through my long hair! I could only stay there on my back and look up at the sky.

The sun was hot, and the light hurt my eyes. I heard noises next to me, but I could see nothing. Then something moved on my foot. It moved over my body and up to my face. I looked down and I saw a man. He was smaller than my hand. Forty more little men followed him.

I cried loudly and they were afraid. They all ran away, and jumped onto the ground. Some were hurt, they told me later. They came back, and one man walked near my face. He threw up his hands and looked up at me. He called, '*Hekinah degul.*' And the other men answered, '*Hekinah? Degul hekinah!*' I could not understand their language.

I pulled very hard and I got one arm up from the ground. I tried to look at this man again. It hurt, because it pulled some hair out of my head. I put out my hand and tried to catch some little men. But they ran away. Then I heard a noise, and something hurt my hand.

'A thousand small swords!' I thought. I looked down. They were arrows! Some arrows went into my clothes and I could not feel them. But other arrows went high into the sky and came down on my face. They hurt me and I was afraid for my eyes.

I put my hand over my face. 'I'll stay quiet,' I thought. 'Then I can break the strings tonight. These people can't hurt me very much – they're too small!'

So I stayed quiet and waited. No more arrows came from the little men, but their noise got louder and louder. 'There are more people here now,' I thought.

I heard a sound near my ear. I turned my head to the noise and saw men next to me.

'They're building something from wood,' I thought. 'It's a

3

I saw thousands of strings . . .

table! Now there are four men on top of it. I understand – they want to talk to me.'

One of the men on the table was older and larger than the other three. He wore a beautiful coat. A little boy, his servant, carried the back of this coat above the ground. The older man called, ' *Langro dehul san.*' Forty people came and cut the strings round my head. Now I could turn and see the people on the table better.

Then the man in the long coat began to speak. He spoke very well, and he moved his hands up and down. I began to understand him. He spoke for a long time. Of course, his words were strange to me, but I watched his hands.

' We will not hurt you,' I understood. ' But do not try to run away, or we will kill you.' I put up my hand and showed him: ' I will stay here.' Then I had an idea. I also put my hand to my mouth: 'I am hungry.'

The man understood me. He shouted to the people on the ground. A hundred men climbed onto my body and walked up to my mouth. They carried food for me. It came from the king, they told me later.

' What food is this?' I thought. ' They're giving me *very* small animals!'

Then I ate a lot of bread. The people watched me with wide eyes because I ate very quickly. A lot of men came with a very big cup of milk. I drank it and called for another cup. I drank the second cup and asked for a third cup.

' There is no more milk in the country,' they showed me with their hands. But they were happy, because I ate and drank their food. They danced up and down on my body and cried, '*Hekinah degul!*'

After my meal, a very important person came to me. He brought a letter from the king. Servants in very fine clothes followed him. He walked up to my face and put the letter near my eyes. Then he spoke, and often turned to the north-west. Their city and their king were there, about a kilometre away, I learned later.

'The king wants to see me,' I understood.

I spoke to this man and showed him: 'Take these strings off me.'

But he moved his head: 'No. We have to carry you with the strings round you. But we will give you food and drink. We will not hurt you.'

I remembered their arrows. 'I don't want to feel them again,' I thought. 'They can carry me.'

The great man went away. After that the people made a loud noise, and they shouted, '*Peplom selan.*' Then they came to my head and cut the other strings. Now I could turn my head more than before. I was happy about that.

I began to feel very tired, and I slept for about nine hours. (There was something in my food, they told me later.)

The people brought some wood and pulled me onto it. Nine hundred men worked for three hours before I was on the wood. I was asleep. Fifteen hundred of the king's largest horses arrived.

After four hours we began our journey. The horses pulled me on my wood, and we travelled for a long time. At night we slept. One thousand men with arrows watched me, so I stayed quiet!

The next day, at daylight, we moved again. In the middle of the day, we were about 150 metres from the city. The king came out. He walked round me and looked up at me carefully.

'Do not climb up onto this man's body!' his men told him. 'It is too dangerous.'

We stopped in front of an old church. This was my house now! The great north door was more than a metre high and nearly a metre wide, so I could go into it on my hands. They put a string round one of my feet and tied it to the wall of the church. I could only walk about a metre away from the outside of my door.

Chapter 2   My Life in Lilliput

Early next day I came out of my house and looked round me. To me, the country of Lilliput was as small as a garden. The tallest trees were about two metres high. I turned and looked at the city. Was this little city a picture in a child's book?

Across the road from my church, about six metres away from me, there was a very big house. I saw people on top of it. The king was there with other men, women and servants.

'They're watching *me*,' I thought.

After a time, the king came down. He got up on his horse and came nearer me. The horse was afraid of me, the man-mountain. It began to jump up and down. But the king – a very good horseman – stayed on his horse. The servants ran to the animal's head and stayed with it.

When he could, the king got down. He walked round me, but he never came too near.

Men brought me food, and the queen and her young sons watched me from the top of the house. After a time the king went away. A number of his men stayed and looked after me.

'Some of our people want to hurt you,' they showed me with their hands. I sat on the ground near the door of my house and tried to sleep.

Suddenly, I felt arrows again and one arrow nearly hit my eye. The king's men caught these bad people – six men – and threw them to me.

I put five men in one hand. I took the other man and put him into my open mouth. He was very afraid. But I laughed and put the six men carefully on the ground again. They ran away from me as fast as they could!

At this time, I slept on the floor of the church or outside on the ground. But the king said to his workmen: 'Make a bed for him.' So they brought 600 little beds to my house and made them into one big bed.

Was this little city a picture in a child's book?

Then the king and his great men met and discussed me.

'Perhaps he is dangerous,' said the first man. 'We cannot untie his strings.'

'He eats too much food,' said the second man. 'The people of our country will be hungry.'

'Let's kill him now,' said the third man. 'We can do it when he is sleeping.'

'No,' said his friend. 'What can we do with his dead body? It is too big.'

Then a man said to the king: 'Some people tried to kill this big man with their arrows, but he was kind to them. He did not hurt them.'

'This is good,' said the king. 'We will not kill him now. But we will teach him our language.'

They did this, and in about three weeks I could speak quite well.

◆

The king often came to see me and helped my teachers. We began to talk.

'Please untie these strings,' I asked him.

'Not now,' he answered. 'But I will think about it. First – and do not be angry – my men will look at your things.'

'I'll happily show your men these things,' I answered, 'but I'll never hurt you or your people with them.'

The next day two men came and walked over me. They looked inside my clothes. They made notes on everything – my notebook, the glasses for my weak eyes, my money and my money-bag.

The king called to me: 'Your sword is as big as five men. Please give it to me. Wait! I will bring more men.'

Three thousand men stood round me and watched.

'Pull out your sword now!' shouted the king.

I took my sword from under my clothes. The sun shone on it and hurt everybody's eyes. I put it on the ground and the king's men quickly carried it away.

'Now give me those other strange things,' he shouted.

I gave him my guns.

After this, the king sent me his 'Rules':

'Follow my rules and we will untie your strings,' he told me.

Rules of Golbasto Momaren Evlame Gurdilo Shefin mully Ully Gue, King of Lilliput, a Great Man.

1 *The Man-Mountain will ask before he leaves our country.*
2 *He will ask before he comes into the city. (Two hours before this, everybody will go into their houses and stay there.)*
3 *He will only walk on the roads.*
4 *He will walk carefully. He will not put his foot on any person, or on their horses. He will not take anybody up in his hands.*
5 *He will help our ships and our men in the war with the people of the Island of Blefuscu.*
6 *He will help our workmen when they build a wall round our garden.*
7 *We will give him food — food for 1,728 of our people.*

The reader will ask: 'Why did the king use the number 1,728?' Well, I was as tall as twelve people from Lilliput. So my body was as large and as heavy as 12×12×12 people from Lilliput — 12×12 is 144; 144×12 is 1,728. This was the answer of the king's clever men.

I read the rules and said to the king: 'I will follow them.'

The next day, men came and untied the strings from my leg. Now I could walk again!

Chapter 3   I Make War on Blefuscu

Reldresal, a great man in Lilliput and a good friend of the king, came to my house with his servant. He wanted to speak to me.

'You can put me on your hand,' he said.

We talked for an hour. 'There are many problems in Lilliput, between the Big-enders and the Little-enders,' he told me. 'The king and most people are Little-enders. But the people of the Island of Blefuscu help the Big-enders here. Now there is war. Can you help us?'

'But what is this war about?' I asked. 'And what is a "Big-ender"?'

'It is about eggs,' answered Reldresal, 'and it is very important. For many years, everybody in Lilliput cut their eggs at the big end before they ate them. We were all Big-enders. But this king's grandfather cut his finger when he opened his egg. He was only a boy at the time, but his father, the king, made a new law. Everybody had to open their eggs at the little end. We had to be Little-enders!

'Many of the king's people were angry and opened their eggs at the big end. Some Big-enders left our island and started new lives in Blefuscu. The Big-enders hate the Little-enders and the Little-enders hate the Big-enders.'

I went to the king the next day. 'I can help you in your war,' I told him. 'The ships of Blefuscu are waiting for the right wind. Then they will come to Lilliput. They know nothing about me because I stay away from the sea. Listen, I have a plan.'

The king listened carefully to my words and he was very happy with my plan.

I then went to our ships and asked questions about the sea between the Island of Lilliput and the Island of Blefuscu.

'It is not more than a metre and a half or two metres to the bottom of the sea,' they told me.

I found some very strong string. Then I left my shoes on the dry ground and walked into the water.

In half an hour I came to Blefuscu and saw their ships. When they saw me, a lot of men jumped out of their ships into the water.

11

I took my string and put it round the front of every ship. Their men sent arrows at me, and the arrows hit my hands and my face. I was afraid for my eyes, so I put on my eye-glasses. Then I pulled the forty largest Blefuscu ships after me through the water. And so I came back to Lilliput.

The king and his great men could only see the ships from Blefuscu because only my head was above the water. But when I came nearer, I called: 'I did this for the greatest King of Lilliput!'

'Thank you,' the king said. 'Will you go back to Blefuscu and bring the other ships? Then I will be king of their country. Its people can work for me and be my servants. I can kill the Big-enders. Then I will be king of the world.'

'No, I won't help you with that,' I said. 'Don't kill those people – it's wrong.'

He was very angry. And from that time, some of the king's friends began to talk about me unkindly.

'Perhaps they'll kill me now or send me away,' I thought when I heard this.

◆

About three weeks later, six important men came from Blefuscu to Lilliput. They wanted to end the war. They brought 500 other men with them – helpers, writers and servants.

The King of Lilliput listened to them. Each man spoke for hours, and then the great men of Lilliput answered – with the help of about 600 men. In the end, the men from Blefuscu and the men of Lilliput wrote their names on a paper. That ended the war between their two countries.

'Don't take too much from the people of Blefuscu. They'll be unhappy again,' I told the king's great men, and they listened to me.

So the King of Blefuscu was very happy. He sent me a letter – he wanted me to visit his country.

Do you remember the Rules of the King of Lilliput? The first Rule said: '*The Man-Mountain will ask before he leaves the country.*'

I knew this rule, but I thought: 'The king won't say no. I won't ask him.' So I got ready for my journey.

That night, one of the king's men – a good friend – came to my house. 'It is dangerous for you now in Lilliput,' he told me. 'The king is afraid. Perhaps you will start another war in Blefuscu and fight us from there. His men want to hurt your eyes. Then they will give you no food. You will die.'

I was angry, but then I thought: 'These people were very kind to me. They're not bad people, only stupid. I'll go to Blefuscu.'

I took the king's largest ship. I put my clothes and my other things in it. Then I walked through the water and pulled the ship after me.

I arrived quickly at the Island of Blefuscu. Near the sea I met two men.

'Where's your city?' I asked them.

They showed me the way. There the King of Blefuscu and his queen came out and met me.

They wanted me to be happy. But there was no big house for me there. I had to put my coat over me and sleep outside on the ground.

Chapter 4   I Come Home Again

Three days later, on the north-east of the island, I saw something in the sea a long way away. Perhaps it was a boat! I walked into the water and went near it. It *was* a boat. The wind and water pushed it and turned it over in the water.

I ran back to the city. 'Can you send 20 large ships and 2,000 men?' I asked the king. 'I want to bring the boat back to the beach.'

The king's ships came. They tied strings round the boat and pulled it nearer the island. Then I took it and turned it up the right way. It was fine.

'Now I can go back to my country,' I cried.

'I do not want you to go,' said the king.

But he gave me food and men. The men helped me, and after two or three days I was ready. I took six animals with me because I wanted to show them in my country. I wanted to take some little people too, but they were afraid.

I left the Island of Blefuscu on 1st May, 1702. On my third day at sea, I saw a ship. I called to her, but nobody answered. Then the ship came nearer and her men saw me. It was an English ship!

I was very happy to see it. I carried my things onto it – I put the six animals in my hat!

One man on the ship was an old friend, Peter Williams. He told the other men my name and everybody was very kind to me.

'Where are you travelling from?' they asked.

I talked about my journeys, and they said: 'These things can't be true. You're ill from your travels.'

So I brought out the little animals and showed the men on the ship. Everybody looked at them with wide eyes. 'Your story *is* true!' they laughed.

I will not tell the reader about that journey, because nothing really happened. One of my animals died, but I sold the other animals in England for a lot of money.

PART 2   GULLIVER IN BROBDINGNAG

Chapter 1   I Come to Brobdingnag

I was rich after my journey to Lilliput, and I bought a house in England. 'I'll live here quietly and be happy,' I thought. But I could not stay there. I went to sea again.

We travelled to the Indies. We bought and sold things there. Near the Molucca Islands, a great wind caught us. Day after day it carried our ship to the east. We had food on the ship, but after weeks in that angry wind, we had no clean water.

Then the wind died and one of the seamen shouted. In front of us we saw a strange country.

Men left the ship in one of the boats, and I went with them. We looked for water, but we could not find a river. We walked for a long time. I went south, but there was no water. So I went back to the boat.

But the boat was not there.

It was on the sea, a long way away, and the other men were in it. The boat moved very fast through the water. I opened my mouth because I wanted to shout to them. Then I stopped when I saw a very big man near their boat. The sea was only half-way up his legs!

I turned and ran away to the mountains. I was afraid for my life.

◆

After a time, I found a very wide road through some trees. I walked on it and looked round me.

'These aren't trees,' I thought. 'It's corn, about twelve metres high, I think. And this isn't a road. It's a way through the corn.'

I heard a loud noise and I was afraid again. Suddenly I saw seven big men next to me.

'They're cutting the corn!' I cried. 'They'll cut me too and I'll die here, away from my dear wife and children!'

15

A man heard me and looked round. Then this big man saw me in the corn. He walked to me and I began to shout loudly: 'His foot is going to kill me!'

The man stopped. For a minute he looked down at me carefully. (We look at a small animal in the same way, and think: 'Will it hurt me?') Then he took me up in his fingers and put me about three metres from his eyes. I was about twenty metres from the ground, so I was afraid.

'Perhaps he'll throw me down onto the ground and put his foot on me,' I thought. 'In our country, we sometimes do that to animals.'

I put my hands up. I wanted to say, 'Please don't kill me!' and 'Your fingers are hurting me!'

He understood. The man turned up the bottom of his coat and put me in there. Then he carried me to the farmer and put me back on the ground.

I spoke to the farmer. He put me next to his ear – about two metres away – but he could not understand me. He answered me, and the noise was as loud as a lot of big guns. I could not understand his words.

The farmer carried me carefully to his house. It was time for the midday meal. His wife cried loudly when she saw me. Women in England do this when they see a rat. Then she began to like me.

She cut up some bread and meat for me. I smiled – 'Thank you' – and took out my knife. Then I began to eat quickly. The people round the table – the farmer and his wife, three children, and the farmer's old mother – watched happily.

A cat jumped onto the table and looked down at me.

'I won't be afraid,' I thought. 'Then this cat won't hurt me.'

I walked past the cat three or four times, and in the end *she* was afraid of *me*!

But then a worse thing happened to me. The farmer and his

For a minute he looked down at me carefully.

wife had a baby, and they showed me to this child. He pulled my body and put my head into his open mouth. Then he threw me down on the floor.

I was now very tired. The farmer's wife took me to her room and put me on her bed. I slept for about two hours – in my clothes, and with my sword.

When I woke, I looked round me. The room was very big – about 100 metres wide and 60 metres high – and the bed was nearly 20 metres wide and about 8 metres from the floor.

Suddenly I sat up, afraid. Two rats were on the bed. They wanted some meat – me! One rat came near me, and I pulled out my sword. The two animals were not afraid. One rat tried to eat my arm, and I cut its stomach with my sword. It died. I could not kill the other rat, but I cut its back.

◆

The farmer's daughter helped me. She was about nine years old and about twelve metres high. But in other ways she was not different from an English girl of the same age. She played with a small house in her bedroom and I slept in the little house away from the rats and other animals.

The farmer's daughter was also my teacher. I showed her things and she told me the words for them. So in one or two days I could ask for everything. She called me *Grildrig*. Then her family used that name, and later everybody in their country – Brobdingnag – called me *Grildrig*. It means a very small man.

The girl looked after me every minute of every day and night. I called her my *glumdalclitch*, my little helper. But in the end I made her very unhappy.

People in the villages near the farmer heard about me and discussed me.

'This animal,' they said, 'is only as big as a *splacknuck*.' (This was an animal in their country under two metres long.) 'But in other ways it is not different from a very small man. It speaks its language, and it is learning our words. It walks on two legs, but its legs are very small and weak. It wears clothes, and it has a very small sword.'

The head man of a village came to the farmer's house because he wanted to see me. I stood on the table and spoke to him. Then the visitor talked to the farmer about me for a long time. Glumdalclitch listened, but she was more and more unhappy. Later, she cried and told me: 'They have a plan. They want to show you to the people of our town when they sell the corn there. Some people will put you in their hands. Perhaps they will hurt you when they do this. My father will make money, but I will try to stop him.'

But she could not stop her father. One day he took me to the nearest town. His workmen made a box for me, with a little door in it. He carried me in this on his horse, and his daughter sat behind him. I had a very bad journey. The horse moved up and down as quickly as a ship in an angry wind.

The town was only forty kilometres away, about half an hour's journey. But I was tired when I arrived. Then the farmer found a room and showed me on a table to about thirty people every time.

Glumdalclitch stood on a chair next to the table and helped me. She asked me questions. I knew the answers now.

'What is your name?' she asked in the language of Brobdingnag.

'My name,' I said in the same language, 'is Lemuel Gulliver.' I had to shout.

'Where do you come from?'

'I come from England.'

'Why are you very small?'

'I am not small. I am as big as the other men in England. You and your people are very, very big.'

The people laughed then. The loud noise hurt my ears and made me ill. Then I had to walk on the table and drink. I pulled

19

out my sword and showed them an English swordfight. And I had to do a lot of other things.

The farmer showed me twelve times that day. After that, and after a very bad journey back to the farmer's house, I was very tired and ill. I did not get better. The farmer wanted more and more money. He began to show me every day at his farm, and people came from a long way away.

Glumdalclitch cried because I was very weak.

'What can I do?' she said.

Chapter 2   I Meet the King and Queen

I was *very* ill now.

'I think he is going to die,' said the farmer. 'I will show him more before he dies. Then I can make more money.'

He began to show me in the big cities. The first was Lorbrulgrud, the greatest city in Brobdingnag. The king lived there. He wanted the farmer to show me to the queen.

'Perhaps the queen will help me,' I thought.

The queen asked me some questions about my country and my travels, and I answered them.

'Would you like to live here?' she asked me in her language.

'Yes,' I answered, 'but I work for the farmer. I'm his servant. I'll have to stay with him.'

'Perhaps he will sell you to me,' the queen answered.

The queen bought me from the farmer for a lot of money.

'Can his daughter work for you?' I asked the queen. 'She's a good friend. I don't want to leave her.'

Glumdalclitch came with me and we were very happy.

One day, the queen took me to the king. He was very busy with his books and papers. He looked at me on his wife's hand, but only quickly.

'So you like *splacknucks* now!' he laughed.

The queen laughed with him and put me in front of the king. He asked me some questions and I told him my name and about my travels.

He sent for his men. They watched me, and they talked about me for hours. Then they spoke to the king.

'This thing,' they said, 'is not an animal. It cannot fly or run very fast. It cannot climb trees, or run away under the ground. It is not a very small person because it is smaller than the smallest person in the world. It is a Thing – and nobody planned this Thing. It is a Mistake.'

I spoke to the king.

'I'm not a Thing,' I said. 'In my country there are millions of men and women of my size. The animals, trees and houses are the right size for us. We have our language, our ruler and our laws.'

I told him about England and the other countries of Europe. He listened carefully. Then he sent his men away.

'I want to hear more from this little man,' he told the queen. 'Build a house for him.'

The queen sent for the best woodworker in the country and he made a box for me. He was a very good worker, and in three weeks I had a big room. It was about five metres long, five metres wide, and three metres high. It had two windows and a door. Glumdalclitch could open the top and clean the room. She took my bed out in the morning and put it in at night.

The queen liked me very much. At dinner time I sat at my table on her dinner table. The queen always cut my food as small as she could. Then I cut it again with my knife and ate it slowly.

On Wednesdays nobody worked, and every Wednesday the king had dinner with his family. Then the king liked to have me and my table near him. He asked me questions about Europe and its people, its laws and ideas, and its rulers.

The queen liked me very much.

I spoke to him about our wars, our great rich families, the fights between our churchmen, our rulers and Parliament. The king laughed and made a loud noise.

He said to the queen: 'Now we know that we are stupid! We think *we* are important people. But these funny little people think *they* are important. Perhaps *they* build a lot of houses in the same place and call them cities. Perhaps *they* fight, and say bad things about one friend to another friend. Perhaps they are not very different from other people.'

Of course I was angry.

'How can he say these things about England?' I thought. 'England is a good and great country. We win wars ...'

Was I right when I was angry? To me, these people were not big and ugly and noisy now. Perhaps *I* will laugh at the people in my country when I see them again.

The king was very interested. He often asked for me. I had to talk about my country, and I did that happily.

'My country,' I told him, 'is really three great countries under one great ruler. The three countries are in two islands, but we also have places in America.'

'But there were people in America before the Europeans went there,' he said. 'Why don't these people have an American ruler?'

I tried to tell him the answer to this, but he could not understand.

Then I told him about our English Parliament.

'It makes the laws for our country,' I said. 'There are two Houses in this Parliament. One is the House of Lords.★ Some great families have a place in this House. A father gives this place to his son when he dies. The House of Lords helps the king or queen. It discusses the laws from the other House, the House of Commons.'

The king had more questions. 'How do these men learn about

★ Lord: very important men had the word *Lord* in front of their name.

the laws?' he asked. 'It is difficult work. They have to know that a law is good for the country – and not for them. Do they learn these things when they are boys, or young men?'

'No,' I answered. 'They learn when they go to the House of Lords. Before that, they learn to kill animals, and they learn to fight.

'The House of Commons is very different. The people of the country send men to it, and those men speak for them. Nobody pays them, but they want to help people.

'A new law first goes through the House of Commons. Then the House of Lords discusses it. Sometimes, the ruler wants more money from the people, and then he has to ask the House of Commons.'

'How can the men in the House of Commons do this work for no money?' the king asked again and again. 'Perhaps some men are bad! Perhaps they take money from people when they make a law. Perhaps they get more money from the people for the ruler or his friends.'

He did not understand my answers, so I told him other things about my country.

'I do not like,' he said, 'to hear about wars. They cost your country a lot of money. Perhaps, my little Grildrig, you are now better than your little people because you know other places in the world. You are a good man – but sometimes stupid because, of course, your head is very small.'

I was angry. 'We are small people with small heads,' I thought, 'but we know a lot of things in our country. I'll tell him about gunpowder.'

'We have very clever men in my country,' I began. 'They can make a dangerous powder. They push this powder into a long gun. Inside the gun there is a very hard ball. When you put fire near the powder, there's a loud noise. The powder pushes the ball from the gun, and the ball flies out very fast. When it hits something, it breaks it. A ball from the biggest gun will kill a lot of men. Or it will break the strongest wall, or send the biggest ship to the bottom of the sea.'

'Who can make this powder?' the king asked me.

'A lot of people, from good schools,' I said. 'I can make it. I can show your workmen and they can make big guns – perhaps sixty metres long. With twenty or thirty of these guns, you can break down the walls of the strongest town in your country in hours.'

'Stop!' the king said. 'Never speak of these things again! Don't talk about them to me or to anybody in my country. Or you will die!'

'This is strange!' I thought. 'He is a good king, and he understands a lot of things. But sometimes people want changes – and he doesn't want to hurt anybody! What will he do when they don't want a king here?'

'Your rulers, your men in Parliament and your clever men are not working for the people of your country,' said the king. 'A good farmer, with his fruit or vegetables, helps his people better than them.'

Chapter 3   I Come Home Again

After two years in the country of Brobdingnag, the king and queen made a journey to the towns and cities of the south. I travelled with them in my box.

We arrived near the sea. Glumdalclitch and I were very tired after our journey, but I wanted to see the sea again.

'Glumdalclitch,' I said, 'we're tired, but I'd like to be outside. Let's go down to the sea.'

She called a boy. He carried my box, and we went out. The boy was not very careful. I felt more ill than before.

'I'll sleep for a time,' I told Glumdalclitch.

She shut my windows and my door. Then I went to sleep.

Suddenly I woke up, because the box moved. Up and up, and very fast. I moved to a window and opened it. I looked out, but I could see nothing – only sky.

Then I knew.

'One of the country's great seabirds is carrying me away!' I cried. 'When it's near its home, it will break my box. Then the bird will carry me to the young birds for food.'

My box began to move faster and faster – up and down. Through the window I saw two other birds. They began to fight with my bird and it could not carry me.

I fell into the sea with a loud noise and I went down . . . down . . . under the dark water. Then, suddenly, my box came up again to the top of the water and stayed there.

'I'm not dead!' I cried, 'and the water isn't coming in. But what's going to happen to me? How can I get out? Will I die because I'm hungry or thirsty or cold? Will great winds break my box?'

◆

One day, I heard a loud noise. Something pulled my box up about a metre, and I could hear the sound of people. So I shouted in different languages. Something or somebody moved the top of the box, and then I heard, in English, the words: 'Is anybody there?'

'Yes,' I shouted. 'I'm an Englishman. Please help me.'

'Your box is now near our ship,' he answered, 'and one of our men is going to break it. Then you can climb out.'

'No don't, wait!' I called. 'Pull the box out of the water and put me on a table.'

The men laughed. When I was out of the box and in the ship, I understood. They were not bigger than I was!

'Why are you shouting?' asked one man.

'Do you know the country of Brobdingnag?' I asked him. 'There the people are very, very big – more than twenty metres tall. I had to shout, or they couldn't hear me. I was there before my journey in the box.'

'This can't be true,' he said.

So I showed him the things in my box. When he saw a tooth from one of the king's servants, he laughed. It was nearly half a metre long.

'Please can I have it?' he asked.

After that he was kind to me. 'When you're in England again, you'll have to write down your story,' he said.

◆

Then I travelled home to my family. It was strange in a world with people of my size.

'Am I in Lilliput again?' I thought.

I could not see my wife and children because I always looked up at the sky. I had to do this in Brobdingnag when I wanted to see people's faces.

My family and friends talked about me.

'He's ill after his travels,' said one friend.

'He isn't going to sea again!' said my wife.

But I travelled again, and you will read about that journey in my next story.

PART 3   GULLIVER IN THE COUNTRY OF THE HOUYHNHNMS

Chapter 1   Houyhnhnms and Yahoos

I stayed in England with my family for some months, but then I wanted to travel again. I left England in my ship in September 1710. For a month we had a good wind. Then it died and we could not move. The seamen were all ill.

'I have to find more men,' I thought. 'I'll go to the island of Barbados.'

There I found men, but the idea was a mistake. These men, and mine, took the ship. They put me in a small room and tied me to my bed.

'There's a man outside your door,' they said. 'Don't come out or he'll kill you. We have your ship now. So we can fight other ships and take things from them.'

They brought me food and drink and I stayed in that room for a long time.

◆

Then, one day, a great wind took the ship out of our way. In May 1711 the other men saw a beach, and they took me to it in the ship's small boat.

'What country is this?' I asked them. They said nothing and left me there.

I began to walk away from the sea. I had my sword with me, and I was happy about that.

When I came to a road, I walked carefully. I was afraid of arrows. I saw some animals near the road, and other animals up in the trees. They were very dirty and very ugly. The bigger animals had a lot of hair on their heads, their faces and their backs, and on the front of their legs and feet. The smaller animals had longer hair on their heads but not much hair on their bodies. Their hair was different colours – brown, red, black and yellow. I hated these animals. When I looked at them, I felt ill.

I walked again. 'Perhaps I will meet some men and they'll help me,' I thought.

Suddenly, I met one of these ugly animals on the road. He stopped and looked hard at me. This made his face uglier. He put out his front foot and I hit him with my sword.

'You will not hurt me, you ugly animal!' I cried.

I did not want to hurt him too much. But he made a loud noise and about forty more animals ran to him. They shouted at me and made angry noises.

I moved to a tree and stood with my back to it. I used my sword, but some animals climbed up the tree. From there they threw things down at me.

Suddenly the animals all ran away quickly. I left the tree and started on the road again.

'Why are they so afraid?' I thought.

Then I saw the answer to my question.

It was a horse. He saw me and stopped in front of me. Then this horse looked carefully at my face and hands and feet. He walked round and round me. I tried to walk away but he stopped again in front of me.

I put my hand on his back. We do this in England when we meet a strange horse. But the horse did not like it. He put up his left front foot and pushed away my hand! Then he made the sounds of a horse, again and again. But each sound was different.

'Is he speaking a language?' I thought.

Another horse arrived, and the two horses made noises.

'They're having a conversation,' I thought.

I was a little afraid and I began to walk away. But the first horse, a grey horse, made a sound. I understood – he wanted me to stop. The two horses came near me and looked carefully at my face and hands. The grey horse moved my hat with his right foot and it fell to the ground. I put it on again. The other horse – a

He walked round and round me.

brown horse – felt my coat, then my clothes. He hurt me and I shouted loudly: 'I'm an Englishman. Please can I sit on your back and go to a town or village?'

The two horses began to talk about me again in their horse-language. One word made the sound *Yahoo*. I tried to say it too. Then I said it to the horses.

The grey horse said the word again and again. I repeated it, but not very well. The brown horse gave me a second word, a more difficult one: *Houyhnhnm*. I tried it two or three times. The last time was better.

One horse talked to the other horse – about me, I think – and the brown horse went away. The grey horse told me: 'Walk in front of me!' I followed him. Sometimes I walked too slowly and he cried, '*Hhuun, Hhuun.*'

'I'm tired and I can't walk faster,' I showed him. 'Can I sit on the ground?'

Then the horse stood quietly and I sat down.

We travelled for five kilometres before we arrived at a house. I began to look for people.

'They teach their horses well in this country,' I thought. 'Now I'll meet the owner of this fine horse and he can help me.'

But there were no people in the first room of the house – only horses. I followed the horse into the second room, then the third room. I waited for people.

The grey horse made a sound, and a smaller horse and two young horses came. They looked at me.

'This is the horse's house,' I thought. 'The grey horse is the owner, and these are his wife and children. The servants are horses too. But how can this be true?'

The 'wife' looked at me in an unfriendly way. She turned to the grey horse and spoke to him. I heard the word *Yahoo*. He moved his head and said: '*Hhuun, Hhuun*'. So I followed him.

We went to another house, and in it there were three of those ugly, hairy animals. They could not leave because there was strong string round them. The other end of the string was in the wall.

The grey horse called a young red-brown horse (a servant), and the servant untied one of the animals. He put that ugly, hairy animal next to me!

The owner and his servant looked carefully at the animal, then at me. Again, I heard the word *Yahoo*. Then I understood. This ugly animal was not very different from a man! He had front feet and I had hands. My feet and the Yahoo's feet were the same. The horses could not see that, because I wore shoes. Our bodies were the same too. But the horses could not see that because I wore clothes.

The red-brown horse gave me different foods. The Yahoos ate meat, but I could not eat it. It was too hard and dirty. Then the horse gave me horse-food, but it was too dry for me.

'I'll have to meet some men,' I thought, 'or I'll die. And these Yahoos are not men.'

I put my hands to my mouth: 'I am thirsty'. The horses gave me milk. Later I made bread from the dry horse-food. Sometimes I caught a bird or a small animal and ate that. With this food and some fruit from the trees, I lived a very good life. I was never ill on that island.

At night, the grey horse – I will call him my owner – talked to his servants about me. They found a place for me near the horse's house, and not too near the Yahoos. I slept there.

Chapter 2   The Life of the Houyhnhnms

I wanted to learn the language of these horses – the Houyhnhnms. The grey horse, his family and his servants wanted to teach me. Why? Because they wanted the answer to this important question: Can an animal – me! – think?

My owner wanted to learn about me, so he gave a lot of time to me.

'You do not walk on your front feet. Why not?' he asked.

'We call them hands,' I told him,' and we don't walk on them in my country.'

'Your nose is too big.'

'It is the right size for men of my age.'

'The Yahoos work for us on the farm, but they do not work well. Nobody can teach them. You are a good Yahoo. You learn and work well.'

'But I'm *not* a Yahoo!' I said angrily, when I heard this. 'I hate these ugly, dirty animals. You hate them — and I hate them too. Please don't call me a Yahoo!'

My owner wanted to know a lot of things and he asked me a lot of questions: 'Where do you come from? Who taught you to think? Nobody can teach the Yahoos to think!'

'I came over the sea from another country in a ship. You make ships from wood,' I told him. 'The other men on the ship brought me here and went away.'

'It is not possible,' he answered. 'No animal can make something from wood and go across the sea in it. Your words are a mistake.'

I could not understand these last words. Later I understood. There is no word in the Houyhnhmn's language for *untrue*. They use language because they want somebody to understand. When the speaker's words are not true, the words are stupid. They are 'a mistake', because the hearer cannot understand him. So why did the speaker speak?

We talked again and again.

'Who are the rulers in your country?' he asked me.

'You call them Yahoos,' I answered.

'Do you have Houyhnhnms there?'

'Yes,' I said. 'We call them *horses*. There are many horses in my country. Yahoo servants look after them. They give them food and make their beds. We like horses. They are strong and they run well. We sit on them when we travel. And they run and jump for us.'

'How can you use them in that way?' asked my owner angrily.

The Houyhnhnms use Yahoos. They work on the farms. They pull things and carry things. There are houses for them, but the houses are not too near the horses' houses. When they are not working, they stay outside.

The Yahoos love to be dirty, and the Houyhnhnms cannot understand that. Other animals like to be clean. I was clean. In this way I was different from the Yahoos. The Houyhnhnms saw this and liked me for it.

◆

One day, I talked to my owner about the wars in my country.

'We had a long war with another country, France,' I told him. 'More than a million men died.'

'Why do you have wars?' he asked.

'Sometimes the rulers want more cities,' I answered. 'Then a strong country fights a weak country. The winner takes the weak country and then the other people are his servants.'

'But you Yahoos cannot hurt other people with your teeth,' he said. 'Our Yahoos hurt other Yahoos in this way. Your words are a mistake.'

I told him about the guns and gunpowder in my country. 'We can kill a lot of people with one big gun.'

He stopped me. 'I do not like our Yahoos,' he said, 'but they do not think. They are stupid. They fight for food, for the best places or because they want to fight. You Yahoos *can* think, so why do you fight? That is worse.'

'He's calling us Yahoos again!' I thought. 'I'll tell him about the good things in my country.'

So I talked for a long time about our Parliament, our rulers, our laws and our clever men and women.

There is no word for *bad* in the Houyhnhnms' language, but they use the word *yahoo* when a worker is stupid (*hhnm yahoo*), for a child's mistake (*whnaholm yahoo*), for strong winds and heavy rain. They use it when they cut their feet. They use it when they hate something.

The Houyhnhnms teach their young horses well. The young horses have to be clean, friendly and kind, and they have to work hard. They have to be strong and well. Every four years the young Houyhnhnms from everywhere in the country meet for games and running and jumping. When a horse wins, a friend sings a song about him or her.

Every four years, too, there is a Meeting. Then the heads of families talk about the country's important problems.

Chapter 3   I Come Home Again

Three years after I arrived in this country, the grey horse came back from a Meeting. His face was very sad.

He said to me: 'The other Houyhnhnms are not happy. You are better than a Yahoo because you can learn. They know that. But you cannot live in my family because you are not a Houyhnhnm. They are afraid. One day perhaps the Yahoos will fight us, and you will help them. They say you have to leave my house. I do not like this, but please find some wood. Make that thing and travel in it across the sea. We will help you. You have to go!'

I was as sad as my owner. I liked the Houyhnhnms. They were very kind and they were good friends. They love everybody in their country, not only their families. They do not marry for love; they marry for strong children. I wanted to stay there with them.

When I thought about my family and friends in England, I thought: 'In many ways they're as bad as the Yahoos here. I don't like my face or body now. I don't want to go home. I don't want to be a Yahoo.'

I fell down at the feet of my owner. For a time I wanted to die. Then I got up and said, 'I understand. You and the other Houyhnhnms are right. I'm a stupid Yahoo. I'll leave your country.'

'Thank you,' answered my owner. 'You can have two months. Then you will have to go. Which servants can help you?'

'The young, red-brown horse likes me,' I said. 'He and I can build the boat.'

In six weeks we made a light boat from wood. We put food and milk and water into it.

On 15th February, 1715, I was ready. Early in the morning, my owner and his family came down to the water and watched. The grey horse cried and put his front foot to my mouth. When I moved out to sea, I heard the red-brown horse. He called in his language: 'Be careful, good Yahoo!'

◆

I was on the sea for many days. I wanted to go to India, but I could not find that country. I was nearly dead when I saw a ship.

The Yahoos on the ship were good men. But I felt ill when I looked at them. I wanted to jump into the sea.

'I cannot live with Yahoos!' I cried.

But a man stopped me and tied me to my bed.

They spoke to me in the Portuguese language. I know this language well and I could understand them. This was very strange for me.

After two or three days, I began to feel better and I told them about the Yahoos.

'This cannot be true!' they cried.

I was angry. After my time in the country of the Houyhnhnms, I could only speak true words. But they listened to my story again. They thought carefully about it and said, 'This is possible!'

I travelled on this ship to Lisbon. There I found a ship for England.

It was very difficult for me. I had to learn to live with men again. In many ways, they are not different from Yahoos.

'But I don't want to live with Yahoos!' I cried. 'I want to live with good, kind Houyhnhnms. I hate dirty Yahoos! And I hate bad Yahoos!'

My people make me angry when they are unkind to horses. I bought two horses. I understand them well and they understand me. I talk to them every day. They are good friends. I can never forget the wonderful Houyhnhnms.

ACTIVITIES

Part 1 A Journey to Lilliput

Before you read

1 Look at the pictures on pages 4 and 8. Discuss these questions
   with another student.
   a What is strange about the people of Lilliput?
   b What problems will Gulliver have there?

2 Read the Introduction to the book, and then answer the
   questions.
   a Are the stories in this book true?
   b What does Swift want us to think about when we read them?
   c Where was Swift born?
   d Who did the people in his country not like?
   e When did people first read *Gulliver's Travels*?

3 Look at the Word List at the back of the book.
   a Which four words are words for people?
   b Which two things can you use in a fight?
   c Which two words are words for places?

While you read

4 What does Gulliver do first? Number these sentences, 1–10.
   a He puts a man in his mouth.   .....
   b He gives his sword and guns to the king.   .....
   c He puts six animals in his hat.   .....
   d He falls out of a boat.   .....
   e He pulls a lot of ships to Lilliput.   .....
   f He drinks a lot of milk.   .....
   g He reads the king's rules.   .....
   h He visits Blefuscu.   .....
   i He learns the language.   .....
   j He learns about a war.   .....

After you read

5 Why:

    a can't Gulliver stand up after he arrives in Lilliput?

    b does Gulliver put his hand over his face when he is on the ground?

    c do the people watch Gulliver with wide eyes when he eats?

    d does Gulliver sleep for nine hours after he eats?

    e do the people throw six men to Gulliver?

    f do the people untie Gulliver's strings?

    g is Lilliput at war with Blefuscu?

    h is the king angry with Gulliver?

    i does Gulliver want 20 large ships and 2,000 men?

    j does Gulliver leave Lilliput?

6 How are these things important in the story?

    a the old church

    b the number 1,728

    c Reldresal

    d eggs

    e six animals

7 Discuss these questions with another student.

    a Who do you like more – the King of Lilliput or the King of Blefuscu? Why?

    b Are the people of Lilliput bad or stupid? Why?

    c What does Swift want to teach us about life in this story?

Part 2   Gulliver in Brobdingnag

Before you read

8 Look at the pictures on pages 17 and 22. How will Brobdingnag be different from Lilliput? Will it be more dangerous for Gulliver? Why (not)?

9 Which is the right word?

  a Gulliver is afraid because men are cutting *corn / trees*.

  b The farmer's wife *cries / laughs* loudly when she sees Gulliver.

  c Gulliver is afraid of a *cat / rats*.

  d Glumdalclitch is the farmer's *daughter / wife*.

  e The farmer *gives / sells* Gulliver to the queen.

  f Gulliver has dinner with the king every *day / week*.

  g The king thinks that Gulliver is sometimes *bad / stupid*.

  h The king thinks that guns are a *good / bad* idea.

  i The king thinks that England is *better / worse* than Brobdingnag.

  j When Gulliver wakes up in the box, he is in the *sea / sky*.

After you read

10 Who or what:

  a puts Gulliver in his coat?

  b is as loud as big guns?

  c is afraid of Gulliver?

  d does Gulliver kill?

  e teaches Gulliver new words?

  f is a *splacknuck*?

  g makes Glumdalclitch unhappy?

  h makes Gulliver happy?

  i can send big ships to the bottom of the sea?

  j does Gulliver show the men on the ship?

11 Who says or thinks these things? What do the words in *italics* mean?

  a '*They* have a plan. *They* want to show you to the people of our town.'

  b 'I think *he* is going to die. I will show *him* more before *he* dies.'

  c '*She*'s a good friend. I don't want to leave *her*.'

  d '*It* is a Mistake.'

  e 'A father gives *this place* to his son when he dies.'

  f 'Nobody pays *them*, but *they* want to help people.'

  g 'Never speak of *these things* again!'

  h 'Please can I have *it*?'

12 Discuss these questions with another student.

    a What does the king think about:
- The English Parliament?
- wars?
- guns?

    Is he right? Why (not)?

    b Why does the king say, 'Now we know that we are stupid!'?

    c What can we learn about life in this story?

13 Work with another student. Have this conversation.

    Student A: You are Gulliver after you arrive home. You want to go to sea again. Tell your wife why.

    Student B: You are Gulliver's wife. You don't want your husband to go to sea again. Tell him why.

Part 3   Gulliver in the Country of the Houyhnhnms

Before you read

14 This story is about horses. Discuss these questions.

    a How do people use horses in your country?

    b Is a horse's life good or bad?

While you read

15 Are these sentences about Houyhnhnms right? Write Yes or No.

    a They climb trees. ....

    b They live in houses. ....

    c They wear clothes and shoes. ....

    d They eat meat. ....

    e They can build ships. ....

    f They have no word in their language for *mistake*. ....

    g They are kind and friendly. ....

    h They can sing. ....

    i They marry for love. ....

    j Gulliver is sad when he leaves them. ....

After you read

16 Are these things strange for Houyhnhnms? Why (not)?

    a dirty, ugly animals with hair of different colours

    b Gulliver's nose

    c Gulliver's conversation

    d the word *untrue*

    e horses in England

    f wars

    g fights for food

    h songs

    i family love

17 Finish these sentences.

    a Gulliver goes to Barbados because ...

    b The Yahoos run away because ...

    c The grey horse pushes away Gulliver's hand because ...

    d The grey horse's wife is unfriendly to Gulliver because ...

    e Gulliver cannot eat the horse-food because ...

    f Gulliver is angry because ...

    g The grey Houyhnhnm is angry because ...

    h The Houyhnhnms like Gulliver because ...

    i The Houyhnhnms have a Meeting every four years because ...

    j Gulliver has to leave because ...

18 Work with another student. Gulliver is on the ship to Lisbon after his visit to the Houyhnhnms. Have this conversation.

    Student A: You are Gulliver. Tell a man on the ship about the country of the Houyhnhnms.

    Student B: You are a seaman on the ship. Ask Gulliver questions. What do you think of his story? Tell him.

19 Discuss these questions with another student.

    a What does Swift want to teach us about life in the story? Do you think he is right?

    b Can people stop having wars? Why (not)?

Writing

20 You work for a newspaper. Write about the war between the Island of Lilliput and the Island of Blefuscu.

21 You are the King of Blefuscu. Write a letter to Gulliver. Thank him for his help. Invite him to visit your country.

22 You are Glumdalclitch. Write about your time with Gulliver.

23 You are Gulliver. Write a letter to Glumdalclitch after you go back to England. Tell her about your journey home from the time when you fell asleep by the sea.

24 You are the grey Houyhnhnm. You don't want Gulliver to leave. You want to talk about this at the Meeting. What will you say? Write ten sentences.

25 Life is often dangerous for Gulliver on his journeys. Write about five dangerous times.

26 Write about one country in the book. How is it the same as your country? How is it different?

27 You work for a holiday company in one of the countries in the book. You want people to visit your country. Write about it for a magazine. Why will this be the best holiday of their life?

Answers for the Activities in this book are available from the Penguin Readers website. A free Activity Worksheet is also available from the website. Activity Worksheets are part of the Penguin Teacher Support Programme, which also includes Progress Tests and Graded Reader Guidelines. For more information, please visit: www.penguinreaders.com.